GIFTED & TALENTED®

*To develop
your child's gifts
and talents*

PHONICS

A Workbook for Ages 6-8

Written by Martha Cheney
Illustrated by Kerry Manwaring

Lowell ⌂ House
Juvenile
Los Angeles

CONTEMPORARY BOOKS
Chicago

Requests for such permissions should be addressed to:
Lowell House Juvenile
2029 Century Park East, Suite 3290
Los Angeles, CA 90067

Lowell House books can be purchased at special discounts when ordered in bulk for premiums and special sales. Contact Department JH at the above address.

Manufactured in the United States of America

ISBN: 1-56565-366-1

10 9 8 7 6 5 4 3

GIFTED & TALENTED® WORKBOOKS will help develop your child's natural talents and gifts by providing activities to enhance critical and creative thinking skills. These skills of logic and reasoning teach children **how** to think. They are precisely the skills emphasized by teachers of gifted and talented children.

Thinking skills are the skills needed to be able to learn anything at any time. Unlike events, words, and teaching methods, thinking skills never change. If a child has a grasp of how to think, school success and even success in life will become more assured. In addition, the child will become self-confident as he or she approaches new tasks with the ability to think them through and discover solutions.

GIFTED & TALENTED® WORKBOOKS present these skills in a unique way, combining the basic subject areas of reading, language arts, and math with thinking skills. The top of each page is labeled to indicate the specific thinking skill developed. Here are some of the skills you will find:

- Deduction—the ability to reach a logical conclusion by interpreting clues
- Understanding Relationships—the ability to recognize how objects, shapes, and words are similar or dissimilar; to classify or categorize
- Sequencing—the ability to organize events, numbers; to recognize patterns
- Inference—the ability to reach a logical conclusion from given or assumed evidence
- Creative Thinking—the ability to generate unique ideas; to compare and contrast the same elements in different situations; to present imaginative solutions to problems

GIFTED & TALENTED® WORKBOOKS have been written by teachers. Educationally sound and endorsed by leaders in the gifted field, this series will benefit any child who demonstrates curiosity, imagination, a sense of fun and wonder about the world, and a desire to learn. These books will open your child's mind to new experiences and help fulfill his or her true potential.

How to Use **GIFTED & TALENTED® PHONICS WORKBOOKS**

This book is designed to give children an opportunity to play with and explore the sounds of the letters of the alphabet. This study of the letter sounds is known as **phonics.**

Almost every page asks the child to write or draw in response to the challenge or question presented. This helps to put the task of working with letters in context. The importance of phonics lies in its ability to help us to understand and express language, so in addition to decoding, the child is expected to demonstrate understanding and practice expression. If this proves difficult for your child, don't be afraid to help. Encourage him or her to talk through the responses while thinking them through. If your child has not yet mastered writing, allow him or her to dictate longer answers while you write them. Write slowly, and let your child watch as you form the letters. Together, read back your child's own words.

The activities should be done consecutively, as they become increasingly challenging as the book progresses. Notice that on many pages, there is more than one right answer. Accept your child's response and then challenge him or her to come up with another. Also, where the child is asked to write, remember that the expression of his or her ideas is more important than spelling. At this age, the child should be encouraged to record the letter sounds that he or she hears without fear of mistakes. This process is known as **invented spelling.** If children only write words they know they can spell correctly, they will limit their written expression. Using invented spelling permits your child's spoken vocabulary to be available to him or her for writing. This vocabulary is vastly greater than the list of words that a five- or six-year-old can spell correctly.

For example, if your child writes *dnosr* for *dinosaur*, that's okay! Praise your child for the sounds he or she heard. You can encourage the child to listen for the missing vowels as you say the word and write it out so that the child can see the correct form. Just keep the emphasis on his or her success—the letters your child did hear— and not on his or her "error." The youngster needs to grow in confidence and exhibit curiosity about the sounds of the letters and how they go together to make words. The experience of attempting new words requires careful thought about the sounds of the letters and makes them more and more the explorer's own.

Reference charts depicting the sounds of letters appear on the next few pages. Help your child use the charts whenever he or she needs a reminder.

Consonant Chart

b banana

h hat

c cat

j jar

d dog

k kite

f fish

l lion

g girl

m moon

n nest

p penguin

q queen

r raccoon

s sun

t telephone

v violin

w wagon

x X ray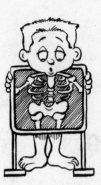

y yarn

z zebra

Vowel Chart

Short Vowel Sounds at the Beginning of Words	Long Vowel Sounds at the Beginning of Words

a apple

a acorn

e elephant

e eagle

i iguana

i ice

o octopus

o ocean

u umbrella

u unicorn

Vowel Chart

| Short Vowel Sounds Within Words | Long Vowel Sounds Within Words |

a cat  **a** cake

e bed  **e** jeep

i pig  **i** bike

o fox  **o** boat

u bug  **u** cube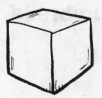

Letter Combinations Chart

Some of the Most Frequently Used
Letter Combinations

bl blocks

br bread

ch cherries

cl clock

cr crown

dr drum

fl flag

fr frog

gl glove

gr grass

pl plate

pr pretzel

sh shoe

sk skunk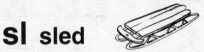

sl sled

sn snow

sp spider

st stop

sw swing

th thumb (sometimes **th** has a harder sound: this, that, the)

tr tree

wh whale

They Go Together!

Each box contains a list of words that begin with the same letter. The words name objects that are alike in some way. Add as many more objects as you can think of to each list. Make sure each addition belongs with the others.

moose   _____
man   _____
mouse   _____
monkey   _____

Explain how these objects are alike: _____
_____
_____
_____

corn   _____
carrot   _____
cucumber   _____

Explain how these objects are alike: _____
_____
_____
_____

They Go Together!

Each box contains a list of words that begin with the same letter. The words name objects that are alike in some way. Add as many more objects as you can think of to each list. Make sure each addition belongs with the others.

ball _____

bat _____

balloon _____

Explain how these objects are alike: _____

_____

_____

_____

policeman _____

pirate _____

pilot _____

Explain how these objects are alike: _____

_____

_____

_____

Mystery Letters

Use the same letter combination to fill in each blank in the sentence below. Do the same for the other sentences.

We can __ __are the fi__ __.

_____

Please __ __ing your __ __other to the party.

_____

__ __y to play the __ __umpet while you ride the __ __icycle.

Mystery Letters

Use the same letter combination to fill in each blank in the sentence below. Do the same for the other sentences.

__ __ich kind of __ __ale is usually __ __ite?

_____

I would like a __ __eese sandwi__ __ and some

__ __erries for lun__ __.

_____

Bo__ __ of us __ __ought we heard a __ __ump.

Mystery Letters

Use the same letter combination to fill in each blank in the sentence below. Do the same for the other sentences.

The __ __ond boy __ __owing bubbles wore a __ __ue shirt and __ __ack shoes.

Sarah __ __ayed with the __ __ane while she ate a __ __um.

The __ __ea __ __ung himself across the __ __oor and did a __ __ip.

Mystery Letters

Use the same letter combination to fill in each blank in the sentence below. Do the same for the other sentences.

Daniel and his __ __other had __ __own __ __ead and __ __occoli for lunch.

_____

The __ __een plant __ __ows out of the __ __ound.

_____

The __ __agon __ __ank a soda while he played the __ __ums.

_____

Calling All Vowels

Fill in the blank spaces with long and short vowels. Make sure the words you form make sense in the story! Add a sentence of your own to finish the story. Draw a picture to illustrate your ending.

J__n and T__m found a b__x. They opened the l__d and peeked __n. The tw__ k__ds could n__t believe wh__t they s__w. __t the bottom of the b__x there w__s a n__st. S__tting __n the n__st was a gigantic __gg. __s they w__tched, the __gg b__gan to sh__ke and sh__ver.

_____

_____

_____

Calling All Vowels

Fill in the blank spaces with long and short vowels. Make sure the words you form make sense in the story! Add a sentence of your own to finish the story. Draw a picture to illustrate your ending.

Laura and Tricia w__nt f__shing wh__n the s__n was j__st c__ming __p. They d__g some w__rms out of the d__rt in the g__rden. They p__cked a l__nch to eat at n__ __n. They p__t on their h__ts and w__lked d__wn to the str__ __m. As soon as Laura put her l__ne in the w__ter, a f__sh began to t__g at it. The p__le began to b__nd.

_____

_____

_____

Calling All Consonants

Fill in the blank spaces with consonants. Make sure the words you form make sense in the story! Add a sentence of your own to finish the story. Draw a picture to illustrate your ending.

Sue and Josh __anted to __ake a __ake. They __ot out __ilk, egg__, __ __our, __ugar, __anilla, and __aking pow__er. They foun__ a __ __eat __ig __owl. They mi__ed e__erything __ogether in the bow__ and __oured the __atter into a __an. They pu__ the __an in the ove__ and __aited.

_____

_____

_____

_____

Calling All Consonants

Fill in the blank spaces with consonants. Make sure the words you form make sense in the story! Add a sentence of your own to finish the story. Draw a picture to illustrate your ending.

One __aturday, Gary __ent for a __ide on his ho__se, Shorty. They went up to the __op of the __ountain to ha__e a __icnic lun__ __. Gary __ __ought a __andwich and so__e coo__ies for __imself. He brough__ a ca__ __ot and an a__ __le for Shorty. Whi__e they we__e ea__ing __unch, they hear__ a __oud boo__.

_____

_____

_____

Zoom!

Label each picture on this page. Each word will contain the **oo** sound that you hear when you say **zoom**. Remember, there are several letter combinations that can make the same sound, such as **oo, ue,** and **ew**.

_____

_____

_____

_____

_____

Add two more pictures that belong on this page and label them.

Sail Away!

Label each picture on this page. Each word will contain the **ay** sound that you hear when you say **sail** or **away**. Remember, there are several letter combinations that can make the same sound, such as **ay, ai,** and **eigh**.

_____   _____   _____

_____   _____   _____

Add two more pictures that belong on this page and label them.

Turtle Talk

Label each picture on this page. Each word will contain the **er** sound that you hear when you say **turtle**. Remember, there are several letter combinations that can make the same sound, such as **er, ur,** and **ir**.

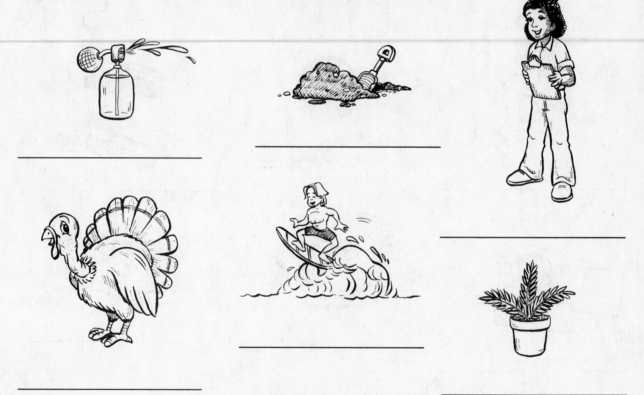

Add two more pictures that belong on this page and label them.

How Now, Brown Cow!

Label each picture on this page. Each word will contain the **ow** sound that you hear when you say **cow**. Remember, there are a few letter combinations that can make the same sound, such as **ow** or **ou**.

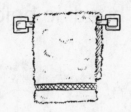

_____

_____

_____

_____

_____

_____

Add two more pictures that belong on this page and label them.

The Sounds of C

The letter **C** has no sound of its own. When **C** is in front of the vowels **i** and **e,** it sounds like the letter **S**. When it is in front of the vowels **a** and **o,** it sounds like the letter **K**.

Look at the pictures on the page. List the name of each picture under the correct heading below.

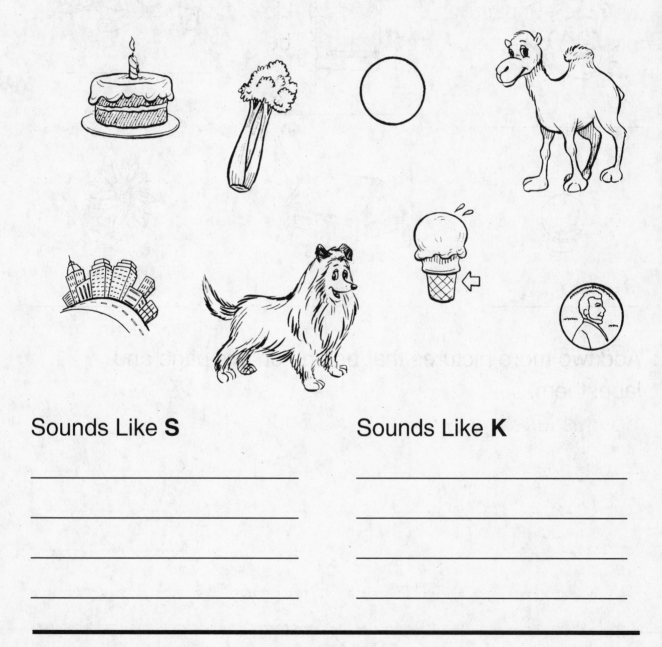

Sounds Like **S**

Sounds Like **K**

_____   _____

_____   _____

_____   _____

_____   _____

The Sounds of G

The letter **G** sometimes borrows the sound of the letter **J**. When **G** is in front of the vowels **i** and **e,** it usually sounds like the letter **J**. When it is in front of the vowels **a, o,** and **u,** it usually sounds like the letter **G**. Can you think of any words that start with **G** that are exceptions to these rules?

Look at the pictures on the page. List the name of each picture under the correct heading below.

Sounds Like **J**

_____

_____

_____

_____

Sounds Like **G**

_____

_____

_____

_____

Tongue Twister

"Peter Piper picked a peck of pickled peppers . . ." is the beginning of a well-known tongue twister. There are many items in the picture below that begin with the letter **P**. Use the lines below to make up a tongue twister using some or all of the words for the items that you found. Add some other words that begin with **P** if you can!

Write your tongue twister here.

_____

_____

_____

_____

Tongue Twister

"She sells seashells . . . " is the beginning of a well-known tongue twister. There are many items in the picture below that begin with the letters **CL**. Use the lines below to make up a tongue twister using some or all of the words for the items that you found. Add some other words that begin with **CL** if you can!

Write your tongue twister here.

_____

_____

_____

_____

Tongue Twister

"How much wood would a woodchuck chuck . . . " is the beginning of a well-known tongue twister. There are many items in the picture below that begin with the letter **V**. Use the lines to make up a tongue twister using some or all of the words for the items that you found. Add some other words that begin with **V** if you can!

Write your tongue twister here.

_____

_____

_____

_____

Poetry Corner

There are many items in the picture below that end with the letters **AT**. Use the lines below to make up a poem using some or all of the words for the items that you found. Add some other words that end with **AT** if you can!

Write your poem here.

_____

_____

_____

_____

Poetry Corner

There are many items in the picture below that end with the letters **OLD**. Use the lines below to make up a poem using some or all of the words for the items that you found. Add some other words that end with **OLD** if you can!

Write your poem here.

_____

_____

_____

_____

Poetry Corner

There are many items in the picture below that end with the letters **AIL**. Use the lines below to make up a poem using some or all of the words for the items that you found. Add some other words that end with **AIL** if you can!

Write your poem here.

_____

_____

_____

_____

Poetry Corner

There are many items in the picture below that end with the letters **IN**. Use the lines below to make up a poem using some or all of the words for the items that you found. Add some other words that end with **IN** if you can!

Write your poem here.

_____

_____

_____

_____

Read and Draw

Read the sentences below. Complete the picture using the information in the sentences. Look for a silent letter in each underlined word! Circle all the silent letters.

<u>Two</u> little <u>ghosts</u> went for a <u>walk</u> in the darkest <u>hour</u> of the <u>night</u>. They saw a <u>bright</u> <u>light</u> shining from a <u>house</u>, so they went up to the door and turned the <u>knob</u>.

What happened next? Write your answer below. Try to use some words that have silent letters.

_____

_____

_____

_____

Read and Draw

Read the sentences below. Complete the picture using the information in the sentences. Look for a silent letter in each underlined word! Circle all the silent letters.

Sally said, "I can't do anything <u>right</u> today! I hit my <u>thumb</u> with a hammer. I fell and skinned my <u>knee</u>. I put my shoes on the <u>wrong</u> feet. My socks do not <u>match</u>."

What did Sally say next? Write your answer below. Try to use some words that have silent letters.

_____

_____

_____

_____

Letter-Sound Riddles

I am yummy to eat. I am red and sweet. I grow on trees. My name begins with the same sound as and .

What am I? Draw a circle around me.

Write a sentence about me!

_____

_____

I am a pest. People do not like to have me around. I am small and black. My name ends with a long **i** sound.

What am I? Draw a circle around me.

Write a sentence about me!

_____

_____

Letter-Sound Riddles

I am white. Sometimes I am slippery. Sometimes I am wet. My name has the same vowel sound as  .

What am I? Draw a circle around me.

Write a sentence about me!

_____

_____

I can fly. I come in many different sizes and colors. There are no silent letters in my name.

What am I? Draw a circle around me.

Write a sentence about me!

_____

_____

Letter-Sound Riddles

I am small. I can fit in a pocket. I am usually made of plastic. I am useful! I have a silent letter in my name.

What am I? Draw a circle around me.

      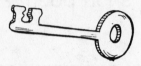

Write a sentence about me!

_____

_____

I have wheels. It is fun to ride on me. I can go fast! My name has the same vowel sound as  .

What am I? Draw a circle around me.

Write a sentence about me!

_____

_____

Rhyming Riddles

I am very beautiful. I come in many shapes and colors.
I am a living thing. I rhyme with   .

What am I? _____

Write a short poem about me. Use some rhyming words!

_____

_____

_____

I am something you eat for breakfast. I am crunchy. I am
brown. I rhyme with something that is part of a fence.

What am I? _____   Draw a picture of a yummy
breakfast. Be sure to include me!

Rhyming Riddles

I am an animal. I lay eggs. I can make a lot of noise!
I rhyme with _____ .

What am I? _____

Write a short poem about me. Use some rhyming words!

_____

_____

_____

I am something you see in the sky. Sometimes I am very bright. Usually you see me at night. I rhyme with something you use to eat soup.

What am I? _____ Draw a picture of me in the night sky.

39

Silent E

Change each word on the list to a new word by adding an **e** to the end of the word. This **e** is silent, but powerful, because it changes the short vowel sound to a long vowel sound. Write a sentence using each pair of words.

Example:

fin   fine

The fin on the fish is in fine shape.

1. hid   _____

_____

2. bit   _____

_____

3. hop   _____

_____

4. pan   _____

_____

5. cub   _____

_____

Silent E

Change each word on the list to a new word by adding an **e** to the end of the word. This **e** is silent, but powerful, because it changes the short vowel sound to a long vowel sound. Write a sentence using each pair of words.

Example:

man   mane

The man held on to the horse's **mane**.

1. Sam   _____

_____

2. spin   _____

_____

3. scrap   _____

_____

4. plan   _____

_____

5. hat   _____

_____

Fractured-Word Puzzles

Fill in the blanks to complete each word. The picture clues will help you. Put the letters from the blanks together to form a new word.

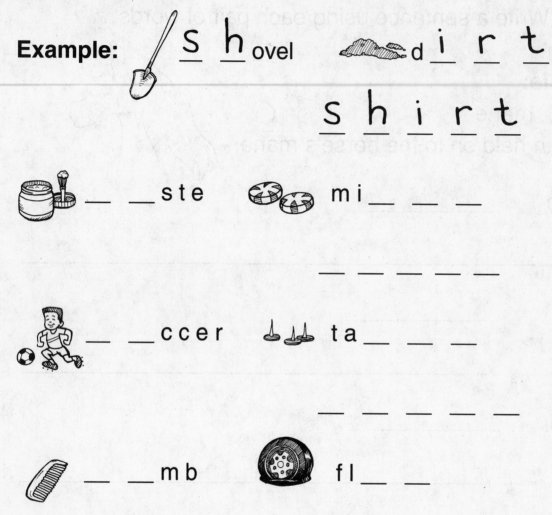

Example: _s_ _h_ ovel   d _i_ _r_ _t_

_s_ _h_ _i_ _r_ _t_

_ _ s t e   m i _ _ _

_ _ _ _ _

_ _ c c e r   t a _ _ _

_ _ _ _ _

_ _ m b   f l _ _

_ _ _ _

Why do all the new words belong together? On a separate piece of paper, make up your own fractured-word puzzle that goes with the other puzzles on the page! Ask a friend or family member to solve it.

Fractured-Word Puzzles

Fill in the blanks to complete each word. The picture clues will help you. Then put the letters from the blanks together to form a new word.

Example: g irl   b o a t

g o a t

_ _ m e   p u _ _ _

_ _ _ _ _

_ _ _ p   c a _

_ _ _ _

_ i m e   t r _ _ _

_ _ _ _ _

Why do all the new words belong together? On a separate piece of paper, make up your own fractured-word puzzle that goes with the other puzzles on the page! Ask a friend or family member to solve it.

Follow the Letter

Make up a "follow the letter" sentence. Make sure that each word in your sentence begins with the letter that the word before it ends with. The first word in the sentence can begin with any letter.

Example:

Th**e** **e**lephan**t** **t**oo**k** **k**ing **G**erald'**s** **s**ilve**r** **r**ing.

Write your "follow the letter" sentence on the lines below. Then draw a picture to illustrate your sentence.

_____

_____

_____

_____

Follow the Letter

Make up a "follow the letter" sentence. Make sure that each word in your sentence begins with the letter that the word before it ends with. The first word in the sentence can begin with any letter.

Example:

Every young girl likes sweet treats.

Write your "follow the letter" sentence on the lines below. Then draw a picture to illustrate your sentence.

_____

_____

_____

_____

Follow the Letter

Make up a "follow the letter" sentence. Make sure that each word in your sentence begins with the letter that the word before it ends with. The first word in the sentence can begin with any letter.

Example:

Put **t**oma**t**o **o**n Nick'**s s**andwich.

Write your "follow the letter" sentence on the lines below. Then draw a picture to illustrate your sentence.

_____

_____

_____

_____

Follow the Letter

Make up a "follow the letter" sentence. Make sure that each word in your sentence begins with the letter that the word before it ends with. The first word in the sentence can begin with any letter.

Example:

How will Lee eat two omelets?

Write your "follow the letter" sentence on the lines below. Then draw a picture to illustrate your sentence.

_____

_____

_____

_____

Hidden Words

In each sentence below you will find a hidden word. All the hidden words belong together. Do you know why? Circle the hidden words.

Example: The little girl ran to her mother.

The car might run out of gas.

My mom gives me some honey every morning.

The address on the letter is 221 Spring Street.

The elevator always gets stuck on this floor.

This is the fourth umbrella that I have broken!

Now write your own hidden-word sentences. Choose any subject you like for your words.

_____

_____

_____

_____

Hidden Words

In each sentence below you will find a hidden word. All the hidden words belong together. Do you know why? Circle the hidden words.

Example: Ta(p **each**) toe twice to keep the beat.

Put the napkin in your lap please.

The little monkey played in the tree.

He should have been home long before now.

These tomatoes are ripe aren't they?

Those dresses are pretty enough for angels to wear.

Now write your own hidden-word sentences. Choose any subject you like for your words.

_____

_____

_____

_____

Word Scrambles

Unscramble each word on the following list. Then write a sentence using only those words. Draw a picture to illustrate the sentence.

shrsoe   _____

rove   _____

teh   _____

lishl   _____

nevse   _____

pallog   _____

_____

_____

Word Scrambles

Unscramble each word on the following list. Then write a sentence using only those words. Draw a picture to illustrate the sentence.

dwnis _____

olcd _____

twnire _____

wobl _____

dan _____

liwd _____

_____

_____

Word Scrambles

Unscramble each word on the following list. Then write a sentence using only those words. Draw a picture to illustrate the sentence.

omse   _____

spinkump   _____

drnclhie   _____

greona   _____

levtew   _____

odfun   _____

_____

_____

Word Scrambles

Unscramble each word on the following list. Then write a sentence using only those words. Draw a picture to illustrate the sentence.

drastuya _____

uro _____

rcdas _____

ylmfia _____

gtinh _____

ydalep _____

_____

_____

Word Pyramid

Complete the word pyramid by writing a new word on each line. Work from top to bottom. The first word you write must have two letters and must include the letter at the top of the pyramid. The next word must have three letters and include both letters from the previous word. The letters do not have to be in the same order. Try to fill in the whole pyramid.

Example:

```
          I

       I     N

    N     I  P

 P     I  N     E

S  P   I   N   E
```

```
          I

       __ __

    __ __ __

 __ __ __ __
```

Word Pyramid

Complete the word pyramid by writing a new word on each line. Work from top to bottom. The first word you write must have two letters and must include the letter at the top of the pyramid. The next word must have three letters and include both letters from the previous word. The letters do not have to be in the same order. Try to fill in the whole pyramid.

Example:

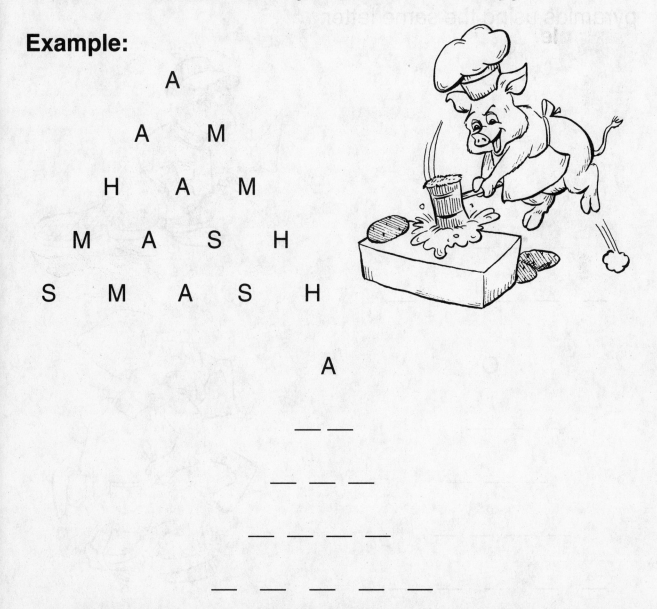

```
          A
       A  M
    H  A  M
 M  A  S  H
S  M  A  S  H
```

```
          A

        __ __

      __ __ __

   __ __ __ __

 __ __ __ __ __
```

Word Pyramids

Complete the word pyramids by writing a new word on each line. Work from top to bottom. The first word you write must have two letters and must include the letter at the top of the pyramid. The next word must have three letters and include both letters from the previous word. The letters do not have to be in the same order. Try to build two different pyramids using the same letter.

O

__ __

__ __ __

__ __ __ __

__ __ __ __ __

O

__ __

__ __ __

__ __ __ __

__ __ __ __ __

Word Pyramids

Complete the word pyramids by writing a new word on each line. Work from top to bottom. The first word you write must have two letters and must include the letter at the top of the pyramid. The next word must have three letters and include both letters from the previous word. The letters do not have to be in the same order. Try to build two different pyramids using the same letter.

E

— —

— — —

— — — —

— — — — —

E

— —

— — —

— — — —

— — — — —

Story Time

Write a story about the picture. Use words with long and short vowels. Try to use words with consonants that look the same but sound differently from one another. Also try to use some words with silent letters.

_____

_____

_____

_____

_____

_____

_____

_____

_____

Story Time

Write a story about the picture. Use words with long and short vowels. Try to use words with consonants that look the same but sound differently from one another. Also try to use some words with silent letters.

_____

_____

_____

_____

_____

_____

_____

_____

_____

Story Time

Write a story about the picture. Use words with long and short vowels. Try to use words with consonants that look the same but sound differently from one another. Also try to use some words with silent letters.

_____

_____

_____

_____

_____

_____

_____

_____

_____

Answers

Page 10
Possible answers include: mongoose, marmot, mole, mink, mule, muskrat

They are all mammals and begin with **M**.

Possible answers include: cabbage, celery, cauliflower, cantaloupe

They all grow in a garden and begin with **C**.

Page 11
Possible answers include: bike, boomerang, book

They are all things to play with and begin with **B**.

Possible answers include: painter, porter, paratrooper, parent

They are all people and begin with **P**.

Page 12
We can share the fish.

Please bring your brother to the party.

Try to play the trumpet while you ride the tricycle.

Page 13
Which kind of whale is usually white?

I would like a cheese sandwich and some cherries for lunch.

Both of us thought we heard a thump.

Page 14
The blond boy blowing bubbles wore a blue shirt and black shoes.

Sarah played with the plane while she ate a plum.

The flea flung himself across the floor and did a flip.

Page 15
Daniel and his brother had brown bread and broccoli for lunch.

The green plant grows out of the ground.

The dragon drank a soda while he played the drums.

Page 16
Jan and Tom found a box. They opened the lid and peeked in. The two kids could not believe what they saw. At the bottom of the box there was a nest. Sitting in the nest was a gigantic egg. As they watched, the egg began to shake and shiver.

Rest of answer will vary.

Page 17
Laura and Tricia went fishing when the sun was just coming up. They dug some worms out of the dirt in the garden. They packed a lunch to eat at noon. They put on their hats and walked down to the stream. As soon as Laura put her line in the water, a fish began to tug at it. The pole began to bend.

Rest of answer will vary.

Page 18
Sue and Josh wanted to make (bake) a cake. They got out milk, eggs, flour, sugar, vanilla, and baking powder. They found a great big bowl. They mixed everything together in the bowl and poured the batter into a pan. They put the pan in the oven and waited.

Rest of answer will vary.

Page 19
One Saturday, Gary went for a ride on his horse, Shorty. They went up to the top of the mountain to have a picnic lunch. Gary brought a sandwich and some cookies for himself. He brought a carrot and an apple for Shorty. While they were eating lunch, they heard a loud boom.

Rest of answer will vary.

Page 20
moose, stew, glue, broom, root

Rest of answer will vary.

Page 21
eight, play, train, hay, sleigh, mail

Rest of answer will vary.

Page 22
dirt, fern, nurse, squirt, turkey, surf

Rest of answer will vary.

Page 23
towel, house, flower, shout, growl, round

Rest of answer will vary.

Page 24
Sounds Like **S:**
    city, circle, celery, cent

Sounds Like **K:**
    collie, cake, cone, camel

Page 25
Sounds Like **J:**
    giant, giraffe, gerbil, gingerbread

Sounds Like **G:**
    gum, game, goose, guitar

Exceptions: give, gill

Pages 26-32
Answers will vary.

Page 33
Silent letters are:

Two little ghosts went for a walk in the darkest hour of the night. They saw a bright light shining from a house so they went up to the door and turned the knob.

Parent: Picture should show two ghosts at the door. There should be a knob drawn on the door. The picture should be colored to represent night. There should be a light in the window of the house.

Rest of answer will vary.

Page 34
Silent letters are:

Sally said, "I can't do anything right today! I hit my thumb with a hammer. I fell and skinned my knee. I put my shoes on the wrong feet. My socks do not match."

Parent: Picture should show that Sally's thumb and knee are hurt. She should be wearing mismatched socks and shoes.

Rest of answer will vary.

Page 35
cherry
fly

Rest of answer will vary.

Page 36
soap
bird

Rest of answer will vary.

Page 37
comb
train

Rest of answer will vary.

Page 38
flower
toast

Rest of answer will vary.

Page 39
goose
moon

Rest of answer will vary.

Page 40
hide, bite, hope, pane, cube

Sentences will vary.

Page 41
same, spine, scrape, plane, hate

Sentences will vary.

Page 42
paste, mints, pants
soccer, tacks, socks
comb, flat, coat

The new words are all articles of clothing.

Rest of answer will vary.

Page 43
home, purse, horse
lamp, cab, lamb
dime, truck, duck

The new words are all farm animals.

Rest of answer will vary.

Pages 44-47
Answers will vary.

Page 48
arm, eye, head, heel, thumb

The hidden words are all body parts.

Rest of answer will vary.

Page 49
apple, lemon, melon, pear, orange

The hidden words are all kinds of fruit.

Rest of answer will vary.

Page 50
horses, over, the, hills, seven, gallop

Seven horses gallop over the hills is the **best** answer.

Some children may put the words in a different order: Over the hills gallop seven horses.

Page 51
winds, cold, winter, blow, and, wild

Winter winds blow wild and cold.

Or: Winter winds blow cold and wild.

Page 52
some, pumpkins, children, orange, twelve, found

Some children found twelve orange pumpkins.

Or: Twelve children found some orange pumpkins.

Page 53
Saturday, our, cards, family, night, played

Our family played cards Saturday night.

Or: Saturday night our family played cards.

Pages 54-60
Answers will vary.

Other

books that will help develop your child's gifts and talents

Over 6 million sold!

Workbooks:
- Reading (4-6) $3.95
- Math (4-6) $3.95
- Language Arts (4-6) $3.95
- Puzzles & Games for Reading and Math (4-6) $3.95
- Puzzles & Games for Critical and Creative Thinking (4-6) $3.95
- Reading Book Two (4-6) $3.95
- Math Book Two (4-6) $3.95
- Phonics (4-6) $4.95
- Reading (6-8) $3.95
- Math (6-8) $3.95
- Language Arts (6-8) $3.95
- Puzzles & Games for Reading and Math (6-8) $3.95
- Puzzles & Games for Critical and Creative Thinking (6-8) $3.95
- Puzzles & Games for Reading and Math, Book Two (6-8) $3.95
- Phonics (6-8) $4.95

Reference Workbooks:
- Word Book (4-6) $3.95
- Almanac (6-8) $3.95

- Atlas (6-8) $3.95
- Dictionary (6-8) $3.95

Story Starters:
- My First Stories (6-8) $3.95
- Stories About Me (6-8) $3.95

Question & Answer Books:
- The Gifted & Talented® Question & Answer Book for Ages 4-6 $5.95
- The Gifted & Talented® Question & Answer Book for Ages 6-8 $5.95

Drawing Books:
- Learn to Draw (6 and up) $5.95

Readers:
- Double the Trouble (6-8) $7.95
- Time for Bed (6-8) $7.95

For Parents:
- How to Develop Your Child's Gifts and Talents During the Elementary Years $11.95
- How to Develop Your Child's Gifts and Talents in Math $12.95
- How to Develop Your Child's Gifts and Talents in Reading $12.95

Available where good books are sold! **or** *Send a check or money order, plus shipping charges, to:*

Department JH
Lowell House
2029 Century Park East, Suite 3290
Los Angeles, CA 90067

For special or bulk sales, call (800) 552-7551, EXT 112

Handy Worksheet

Note: Minimum order of three titles. *On a separate piece of paper,* please specify exact titles and ages and include a breakdown of costs, as follows:

(# of books) _____	x **$3.95**	=	_____
(# of books) _____	x **$4.95**	=	_____
(# of books) _____	x **$5.95**	=	_____
(# of books) _____	x **$7.95**	=	_____
(# of books) _____	x **$11.95**	=	_____
(# of books) _____	x **$12.95**	=	_____

(Subtotal) = _____

California residents add 8.25% sales tax = _____

Shipping charges
(# of books) ____ x **$1.00/ book** = _____

Total cost = _____